BREAKFAST WITH MY FATHER

BREAKFAST WITH MY FATHER

W. KEITH REED

CONTENTS

To my father
Wendell Keith Reed
Born: Feb 16, 1932
Died: June 17, 1996

PREFACE

My father divorced my mother when I was 5.
Thus began a life-long adventure in looking for and
(mostly) not finding my father.

My passion for writing poetry came as I discovered a
viable tool for processing my anger, confusion, guilt and
fractured self image.

"Breakfast with my Father" began in 2016 as I made my
way from California to Minnesota. On the way to my newly
appointed church music position, I travelled through the
city of my birth, Bismark, N.D., where for the first time, I
visited the house where I had lived.

I visited the church my father had pastored. I visited with
the, now, aged woman who took care of me during the first
two years of my life.

I found myself immersed in the life of my parents; their
thoughts about each other and the decision to grow their
little fractured family.

These poems are my attempt at reconciling the feelings
of a 5 year-old with those of a grown man, father and
grandfather.

This is my pilgrimage. I do not relate actual historical
events or empirical truth.

You are welcome to join me!

THE GREAT KEEPER

A weary traveler, worn, I was
from life out on the road.
The tree said, "Come and find some rest
And let me share your load".

I smiled. The invitation I received
from my new friend that day
came like an evening breeze
and so, compelled to stay,

I ventured close upon its massive trunk
my back to rest.
It was then I saw this special tree,
and thought it best

To point out the unlikelihood
of finding such a tree;
one side alive – the other dead
now how could this thing be?

The natural surge of nutrients
and life-supporting flow,
unencumbered from the root to branch
a healthy tree should grow.

With sunshine and some rain
and ample room for roots to waken,
I marveled at divergent paths
each side the tree had taken.

The symbol of duality
for all the world to see
was emanating from the image
of this fractured tree.

While leaning backward on the tree
I gained a new and clear perspective.
Regarding life and death
there seemed to be a new directive

"Look through your eyes not with them"
said the tree to this illusion.
"It's not dividing death from life, my son,
It's clearly fusion

The space between what lives
and what is dead is thin, indeed,
as you confuse your need for guidance
with your need for speed".

"The part that's dead is useful
in its own way, can't you see?
It's house for guest and ledge for rest,
a complement for me".

"The part of me that lives
has value for a measured number.
A place to play – a place to hide
a place where young ones slumber".

"The part of me no longer living
functions in providing
a stark reminder
where my past and present are residing".

As I'm reminded of my death
I live my life much deeper,
entrust what lives and dies
Into the hands of the Great Keeper.

TO BUILD A WALL

I asked my father
why there was such blood upon his hands.
He looked into my eyes
and said to my surprise,
"That's how they look when you protect your lands".

"You'll understand it better
when you've grown a bit, my son".
"The measuring and tending,
the patching and the mending,
to build the wall one's work is never done".

It seems my pedigree
is filled with builders of the wall.
It was their one solution,
their most treasured attribution.
The duty of each generation's call.

To decline participation
would be deemed a mortal sin.
Each one his own weight bearing,
but the question never sharing
of what the wall should try to keep out or keep in.

"We need to keep our faith
and precious values locked up tight
from those who come to steal,
imagined or for real.
There's nothing left if you're not sure you're right".

And so the men
within my clan continued on to build their wall.
Around the table winking,
heads were nodding, never thinking
that the mortar mixed with fear insured the fall.

I left my clan of builders
or perhaps they just left me.
My father's exclamations
and my heart's own protestations
caused a rift within the wall's integrity.

Breathless then, I billed
my life as one great talent show.
My builder's gift misusing,
still I found it quite confusing
that my passion left me with so far to go.

Looking back
I see so many walls I've left undone.
The need for recognition;
an unstable ammunition
that destroyed each wall before it had begun.

But what is this I see
as I assess the road ahead?
The Masons from the past;
quarried memories come at last and
gather for me all the older stones instead.

From eons past, an ancient knowledge
helps me build my wall.
All are called to build one,
the novice and the skilled one.
Without a wall there'd be no life at all.

The wisdom from the ancients
help distinguish old from new.
The new stones I can feel;
and have so much appeal
might not serve me as the ones that I outgrew.

The wall that I shall build,
will have integrity and strength.
My past walls integrating;
and with grace illuminating where the drawbridge goes,
it's height and depth and length.

MY MOTHER'S WOODS

Whose woods these are
I think I know,
the rootless kind just meant for show,
the kind that as you travel past
would soon convince took years to grow.

Whose woods these are
now let's look close
in vain attempt to diagnose
the fungal sickness at the root;
the remedy too large a dose.

Whose woods these are
the family claim.
No one remembers now the name.
But those who keep the fence repaired
are not the only ones to blame.

Whose woods these are,
brought pride of place,
the form with substance to embrace.
Yet owing to the fallen breed,
could not the father's lie erase.

Whose woods these are
will never see
the desperate inequality
that lay between each grafted branch;
the fight to live, the right to be.

The woods are lovely
but take care,
if you would ever venture there
just watch your step so you don't fall.
The unused paths might need repair.

The woods are lovely
from afar,
Where each and every light a star,
reminding of the vast unknown
are really bugs kept in a jar.

The woods are lovely
so pretend
our sackcloth and our clothes to rend
in hopes that we will soon recover
reasons our lost souls to mend.

The woods are lovely
but you swore
as equal child and hope I bore
the distance would our love renew
but fragile stitches only tore.

The woods are burning
and it's hot.
Remember all the beauty sought
as we would walk along our wood?
Yet grateful to expose the rot.

The woods are burnt.
You've gone it seems,
yet I've had more inside my dreams
than writing you in charred remains
the riddle and then what it means.

The woods look dead
but look once 'round.
The flower rising from the ground
a lily, with three growing stems.
The heart to heal, the meaning found.

THE FRONT DOOR

I have a front door in my house
it's made of tinted glass.
While standing near,
it's not quite clear
you see me when you pass.

The other thing about the door
that pleases me immensely
is that it slides
from side to side
not simply but intensely.

While growing up our houses
all had doors made out of wood.
When people knocked
you thought
you knew exactly where you stood.

You grabbed the knob, turned it,
then stepped back to let them in,
allowing inward access
never knowing
where they'd been.

With good intent and youthful heart
some entered in my home.
The ugly not
an outward spot
but strictly of the bone.

Concluding, then that my position
was so compromised,
an insularly plan
was soon
devised and realized

To see all those who would come in
yet I would not be seen,
the tinted glass
would function
as a large translucent screen.

A chance for me to think as they reviewed
their own reflection;
a little time,
completely mine
to proffer my rejection.

It's not that I hate people
and resent all my connections.
I like to see,
ahead of me,
all possible rejections.

And so to add provisions
to reduce the needed space,
I slide my door
to open it
and welcome the embrace

Of those, already recognized,
whom through the door I've granted
permission to access
my little world,
askew and slanted.

My goal, transparency,
produces fog at every breach.
The risky space,
to see my face,
the lesson glass doors teach.

My fear, oh God, to open up
to all who would dare enter
a painful cost,
my heart is lost
if you be not its center.

CROSSROADS

I met you at the crossroads
of a town we used to know.
Funny how the ash
from burning dreams resemble snow.

You keep asking for the truth
and all I know is how I feel.
With all the plate glass windows blown
it's hard to know what's real.

The keepers of forgotten dreams
were busy with the fire
and wondered where in all this mess
they'd find another buyer.

For early, we had learned the ways
of how the dreamer thrives.
You close your heart and then your eyes
and pray for eight more lives.

And so decided, though unspoken,
that we'd meet again,
ever as an endless tune
awaiting its refrain.

But now, in whispers, let us speak
so as to not awaken
the giant that we exorcized
that left us deeply shaken.

And viewing, as we walked
the desolation of our dreams,
we turned and smiled as if to say
we now know what it means

when history and purgatory
join hands, in the square
to raise the flag of truce
and find the flagpole isn't there.

We trip and fall on broken pieces
of our loss and pain;
too heavy was indifference
and guilt was too much strain.

.

The walls we built had kept out
what our hearts would fain let in
and doubt had suffocated
all the will to just begin

Coming to and coming from
our travels on this road,
and looking back I recognize
the past bares quite a load.

The pressure of the past to form
and shape my heart's intention
reveals the weakness of my sight
and memory's retention.

Oh great Discerner
of the hidden crossroads of my mind,
as I traverse familiar paths
and those I've yet to find,

hold You tight, while I sift through
the empty ashes of my longing,
to resurrect a simple faith
and in you find belonging.

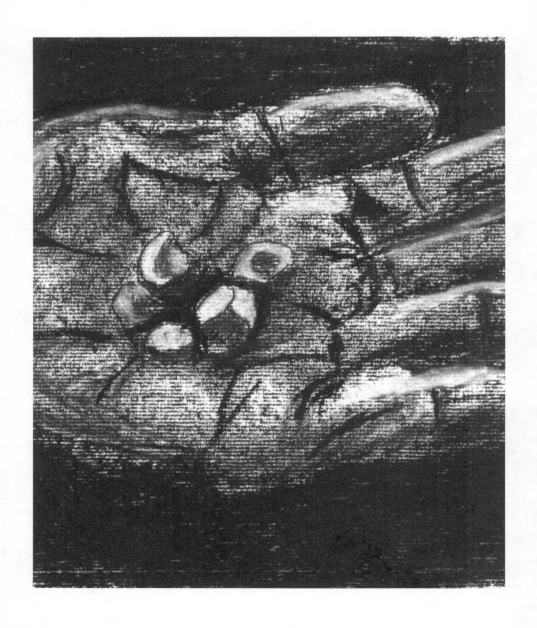

THE PLANTER

She said "let's plant a garden
and we'll make my dream come true.
I've dreamt how I could till
and find the planter man in you".

The newness of the home
and the deepness of the need
would replace romantic images
with hungry mouths to feed.

And so the tall, dark stranger
learning what it meant to wed;
the ring upon the finger
and the ring inside the head,

began to plant and
garner to himself the accolade
of laying with the woman
in the bed that he had made.

His father was a seeder
who despised the dirty nails.
He taught his son to watch
how one man wins and one man fails.

"The time", he said "to tend the field
is only compensated
by understanding that the wind
can be manipulated.

The wind will blow and dust will fly
and lives around will shatter;
the prayers and lamentations
will be simply worthless chatter.

What people need in times of want
is what a seeder knows.
Clutching hands will take the seed
regardless if it grows.

Confuse not, son, the difference
of the planter and the seeder.
The one is meant for dirty nails
the other shows a leader".

She called to him to join her
as she prayed and as she dreamt.
Looking in her eyes
he was confused at what she meant.

The way that she was pointing
led them further from the goal
and so the seedless planter
simply waited by the hole

and placed within it
all the disappointment and the grief.
The crowd would call him hero
but his heart would call him thief.

She wondered if the seed she bore
would help him to recover;
and learn to give to her
what he was giving to another?

And so the life of seedless planters
leads to mindless scraping.
And vain attempts at merriment
reflect the holes that, gaping,

swallow up the fallow
and the long abandoned lands.
Yet, icons of a tortured past,
unchanged by human hands,

are reconstructed and redeemed
the broken hearts to mend
and rain reveals the hidden truth
that only God can send.

TWO LIGHTHOUSES

I live in the house of the Seaman.
He's the captain of a very large ship.
He travels the world,
bringing this,
taking that.
Everyone loves my father the Seaman

And he moves standing still.
The moon seems to pull him,
with his big hand in mine.
And I laugh
at the smell of the salt in his beard.
He brings me fine linen
from faraway places
and I'm an exotic princess
from some land of enchantment.
I love my father the Seaman.

I'm surrounded by images
that fill me with wonder.
All of the possible colors and smells
and the ways of the world
just hang on my wall,

And infuse all my senses

I am lifted in hope
that I am not alone.
And my heart seems to soar
like the sails of his ship –
The ship of my father the Seaman.

And he lifts me at night.
He lifts me up out of my chair
and my face is submerged
in the story of all that I am,
And can be,
and will be.

He looks at me, then,
in the pale lamp light.
And I see through the waves of the wrinkles that
crash on his eyes;
one lighthouse to show me the way,
A second to lead me home.

Wherever he goes, he takes me.
And I sit in the galley,
inside of his heart,
housing all of the meanings and longings
not simply expressed.

I am always with him.
And he carries my heart
as he travels the seas.
And he carries that which he must
only to meet me at a sunset
to carry me home –
where I live in the house of a Seaman.

NIGHTWATCHES

We enter in at dusk
when candles newly lit and glowing
cast intimidating shadows
on symbols rich beyond our knowing.

The evening peace reducing sounds
of people, cattle, fowl
reveals the counterpoint
of angel praise and demon howl.

The crowd, it's night-time vigil
to return to home and fire,
reveals the cosmic dance
that speaks of heavenly desire.

For surely as my father
and his fathers long before
would enter this most Holy Space
and prostrate on the floor

give homage and due service
to the one who dwells in Light.
Entering as beggars,
given grace and given sight.

I've grown into this calling
as I close each door behind me,
Stepping lightly through each chamber
to where God alone can find me.

And lifting holy hands
in praise of him who does what's right,
my vision never clearer
than in the Watches of the Night.

We sleepers of the day
must exercise determination
and balance both
our need for rest and spiritual vocation

The call, it's clear, is not for all
to offer nightly prayer.
The value not on quantity
but quality laid bare.

The craftsmanship of prayer
is once, for all, a slippery slope.
When men are speaking just to men,
men quickly lose their hope.

So we watchers of the night
use fewer words with which to start
this dialogue of heaven
and this syntax of the heart.

Yet, God created night
as more than absence of the day.
The night reveals
what cannot be revealed another way.

We marvel as we witness
in the night creation's splendor.
Accepting in the light
our inabilities to render.

So we see you, Great Creator,
in the day and your provision.
The witness of your sovereignty
at night yields no division.

And in the darkest hours
of the night we find revealing
the questions and the answers;
the destruction and the healing.

Destroy in me the longing for the light
that brings distraction
and heal in me the apathy of night
that yields inaction.

Reflect in me your light
as to your mercy I will cling.
Creator of the Night
come teach my dying voice to sing.

DRAWBRIDGE

I went looking for my father
in the spring of '68
With some sandwiches and clothing
and my life and mother loathing
I met my sister by the front yard gate.

I went looking for my father
with conviction made of stone.
To the school yard brushes fleeing.
An hour quickly passed then seeing
shadows of the evening lead us home.

As far as I can see,
always the back of me
walking on.
Waiting for the bridge to be drawn.

I went looking for my father
in my fantasy and dreams.
Never sure when I awoke
what I mended, what I broke.
A will to pay without sufficient means.

I went looking for my father
in each woman that I hated.
Looking through my broken image
hoped the game was not a scrimmage.
Always drinking and was never satiated.

Then one day I found my father.
He was standing all alone.
The resemblance quite unnerving
and my anger undeserving
asking simply if I wanted to go home.

My father, convalescing,
without the wheelchair or the crutch.
My pain and anger, screaming,
confused the facts for deeper meaning
never knowing that his love could love so much

As far as love can take me;
there to mend me,
then to break me,
sacred scar.

The Drawbridge obsolete.
A brand new pathway to complete
as we wash each other's feet.
The journey may be long
but never far.

BLIND EYES STILL CRY

I was born with no true sense of sight
its when the glare of noonday resembles darkest night
I can't see your wrong and I can't see my right
but all can see that blind eyes still cry

I use my hands to slowly make my way
But what, in hope, I grasp seems so reticent to stay
It's far too hot to stand and much too cold to lay
but there's no missing blind eyes still cry

Eyes, strategically placed inside of me,
like lifeless pools refuse to be
objectified by life's scrutiny

Eyes, that can hear a lie
can also hear as you pass by
and believing you can hear my cry

For Mercy's sake, please see through this mask
and seeing what remains, if it's not too big a task,
hear with my feeble voice what a fainting heart would ask
Does it even matter that blind eyes still cry?

And just to be clear, I've never seen the light
and when the deed's done and you've given me my sight
Don't think me naive as to think all will be right
yet, all will see that new eyes still cry!

THE KNOWING AND BELIEVING

When I set upon a journey
I do my best to plan ahead
check the oil
And the tires
all the coils
and the wires
and fearing not the nighttime drive
I usually choose the day instead

And I'm prone to clean the windows
front and back before I go
I see better
without splatter
and though wetter
still no matter
A safer ride ensures that
what I see is what I know

And since I've no concrete insurance
that I will grasp for what I reach
I will forgo complete assurance
that my ego fain would preach
that I control, somehow, my future
sweet illusion of the patch
with fragile threads I sew and suture
all my fears to faith attach

All the more this trip investing
in the poorness of my state
that with you, at your requesting
something special to create

And so it is with you beside me
I develop other skills
as I steer
and as I'm braking
you draw near
as we are making
plans to parts unknown
the process as our love distills.

It seems I meet you better
in the nighttime driving hours
less to see
more to feel
room to be
trusting real
and reaching for the hand
Trusting images the sunlight soon devours.

And when I struggle to decide
Upon which path to travel
the nighttime hours soon provide
the license to unravel

parts of our bold tapestry
that loving hands are weaving
As God produces in our hearts
the Knowing and Believing.

THE LOCKSMITH

A man came by the house the other day
Resembling Peter Lorre
in a Karloff sort of way
Asking what the hell he wanted
as I kept my fear at bay
He said that he had come to fix the locks

Our house sure needed help that much is true
A witness to the crime
before Korea, '52
Of certain houses that were built
with stones and timber no one knew.
He asked if he could come and fix the locks

I've never met a locksmith or I have no recollection
To life of crafting keys
to open doors I've no objection
But looking at this man
I made an untoward connection
That he was coming here to fix the locks

I asked him in and offered him a seat
It was then I noticed that
there were no shoes upon his feet
One minute more and then
our salutations were complete
He was anxious to begin to fix the locks

He stood and from his pocket pulled a pouch
Removing two small wires
left the pouch upon the couch
And walking to the front door
with no hint of bend or slouch
He knelt upon the floor to fix the locks

Into the lock he slipped the two small wires
And suddenly, from out his pocket,
pulled what looked like pliers
And then what happened next
from you such trust and faith requires
The man began to sing into the lock.

The sight that I beheld defies description.
The pliers seem to have the etching's
of some strange encryption.
The likes of which I've only seen
in late night science-fiction.
There seemed to be more to this man than locks

He turned to look at me and started crying.
"These doors", he said "had come from
rooms with little children dying".
He heard them as he sang
and with a loving voice replying
"I'm here to set you free from doors that lock".

"I contracted as a young man scarlet fever"
"To keep me from the war
my father used it as a lever
And living in such shame
I viewed myself as a deceiver".
"I turned to fixing other peoples locks"

"I heard the voices calling right away.
The hurting and the broken
simply begging me to stay.
And I convinced myself
that I might truly find a way
To save the lives contained behind these locks"

"All your doors are really fine" he said.
"All you need to do is
simply get it in your head
That broken locks are broken
due to broken lives instead.
It's really inside out to fix a lock."

"Come and let me teach this song to you.
The melodies can only
be retained by just a few.
It takes away your need to look
and helps you just see through.
See yourself inside the broken lock."

My life has really never been the same.
I gained a new perspective
on the day the locksmith came.
The song I learned to sing
releases all my guilt and shame.
I have an answer for each broken lock.

WHO CAN SAY?

Would the painting be so clear,
reflecting and describing,
were not the passion and the fear
a tool of Love's prescribing?

Who guides the brush along its course
each reflex and decision
that shows the scalpels loving Source
or self-indulged incision?

Who can say?

Is this small gift I bring today,
a token of my pleasure,
redeemed by some sweet word you say
or victim of your measure?

Can what I mean and I intend
exist without approval,
the constant rip of what I mend,
collection and removal?

Who can say?

Can I the sun's most glorious beams
somehow manipulate
or setting glass before my eyes
another world create?

While looking at my painting
on the wall I am offended
and you find
deeper meaning to it all
than I intended?

Does your perception validate
and give my work true meaning
or do you simply animate
a truth within me dreaming?

Who can say?

Can I mix the who I am
With all I'm meant to be?
Combining ounces with the gram
reveals complexity

Can I embrace the air and find not
my own arms enfold me
or know the one who's there
and understands me –
still will hold me?

Who can say?

FOOL OF THE MOON

There you hang in a dark blue sky
keeping count of who live or die.
You make the rounds and you make your pull
filling in the space till you make it full.

Your pockmarked face and your toothless grin
oozing through the space of my secret sin.
Etching my disgrace on your lifeless skin.

I'm just another fool of the moon.

You have no strength. You have no light.
You're only seen coming out at night
with some coward's laugh and a twisted smile
lighting every curve, every senseless mile

on this mountain road, as I'm flying blind.
While the shifting load of my reckless mind
Imitates the code father left behind.

I'm just another fool of the moon.

The genetic swirl that undoes my heart
undermines my head tearing me apart.
No one to blame so I blame myself
watching 8 by 10's falling from the shelf.

The circled glow in the pirate dust
lets the seekers know while I polish rust
that the evening show will confirm their trust.

I'm just another fool of the moon.

So, I lift this cup and I lift this plate.
Accept the pain as I deny the weight.
Let the sun remind me of moments lost
as I check the ledger and review the cost.

With holes in hand and a mindful look
you will help me stand and re-write my book
and to heal my land which I long forsook,

you will save another fool of the moon.

MOUNTAIN LAUREL

While walking in the mountain mist
I came upon a Glen,
a hallowed, early morning tryst
of wealth beyond my ken.

Amid the bramble and decay
of life amid the pines,
there strewn the ravishing array
my captured heart enshrines.

For as a drink is offered
to some parched and weary soul,
the earnest vision proffered
did extract a painful toll.

Amid the intersection
of the Holy and mundane,

providing such reflection
as to make all else profane,

the purest genuflection
of my pleasure and my pain.

With my Mountain Laurel, I find peace.

My Laurel of the valley
caught my eye one summer's day.
Not prone to whim or dally,
I advanced amid the fray.

Surrounded by her suitors
I remember, on reflection,
communal prosecutors
and their whispering objection.

Returning from the war
I, too, had felt the scorn collective.
The village honor soon
replaced with fears most stout, infective.

For what one thought to understand
then found it not to be
reflects the deeper contraband,
once treasured, now debris.

So with my tarnished vision
I approached my prime directive;
communal circumcision,
both, redeeming and corrective.

While tending hearth and home
and all that life with me demanded
her heart began to roam,
receding trust, as fear expanded.

Sitting in the evening glow,
her fingers always knitting,
praying just to stem the flow
of judgement unremitting.

Despite the trend,
I sought to build a house in which to thrive;
the urge to mend,
the fragile cords that kept our love alive;
no will to bend,
no pretext to pretend or to contrive,

with my Valley Laurel I'm undone

Remind me, blessed mountain,
as you rise above my sight,
with every stream and fountain
and with every bird in flight,

that what I see
is only part of some amazing story.
The truth in me
resides not in some transit allegory.
The Laurel Tree,
The wealth of God, this small depository;.

With my Mountain Laurel, I find God

THREE LEAVES

A faint yet vivid sound of scratching
somewhere on the roof
refused to yield, so to the backyard porch
in search of proof

I ventured out as waning sunshine
sliced the leafless trees.
The lustful dance of winter
pirouetting in the breeze.

Expecting confirmations
of a rodent or some bird
to justify the unknown sound,
I found it quite absurd

to witness the intent
of some illusionary skill,
inserting three large leaves
between the window and the sill.

Each leaf, all by itself,
would hardly merit such attention,
combining them
necessitates their honorable mention.

The irony that you were on my mind
as winds were blowing
three large leaves and, yet
arranging them without my knowing,

In such a tiny space
outside my window in vibration.
The brevity of nesting
juxtapose to long migration.

For, surely, this first leaf
with all its power from the tree,
instructs the other two
in all the ways that they should be.

The anger and confusion
gives this rigid leaf a grace;
allowing other leaves from other trees
to find a place.

The second leaf, of milder stock,
committed to the serving,
a reminder of the focus
when the fear becomes unnerving.

Thus, resonating with the two,
the third absorbs the shock
when horns of fear and
horns of purpose ultimately lock.

And in the dance that leaves rehearse
when from the tree they fly,
the third leaf gently illustrates
its graceful way to die.

The scraping that I heard
outside my window just today
was all the colors of your life
united just to say

that all the seasons of your times
had meaning but in tandem.
The measured and the honored
through the lens of chance and random.

And I, between the space
of who you were and who you are,
can see that, though you've grown,
The growth is deep and not so far.

So we hold you as we hold ourselves
and pray for truth and meaning.
The confidence in foolishness;
the strength to stand in leaning.

I'd like to say much more
as I'm concerned you haven't heard.
Simply hoping what I'm feeling
might be clearer as a word.

But I will know that He, who knows
and holds your ravaged heart,
binds all things unto Himself;
each ending and each start.

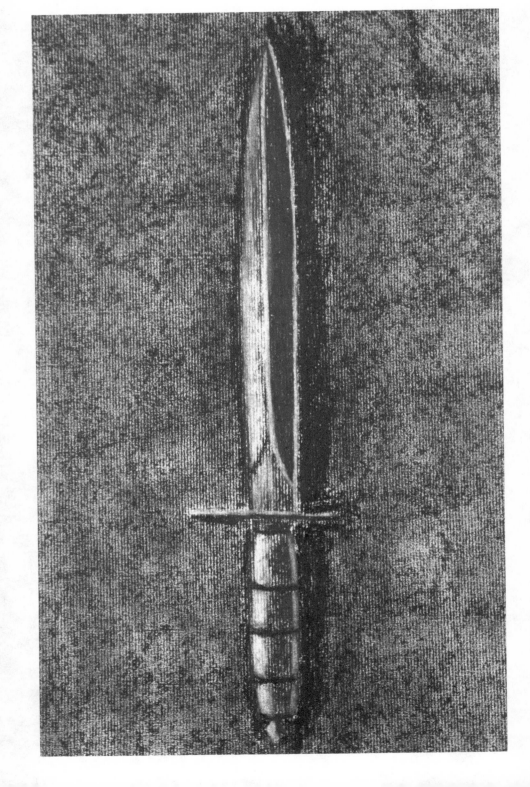

THE THREEFOLD HEALING

The initial wound came as
life formed deep inside
and elaborate frames hide who
spoke truth and who lied

But the wall has been breached;
no reversing the course
of one sermon twice preached,
Illuminating the source.

But delivery was made in
a hailstorm of guilt.
Embryonic brocade graced
the encompassing quilt.

And the wounded one kept the
eternal appointment
and the grieving one slept
misapplying the ointment

that should have reversed
the degenerate spore
of the fatherless curse at
the fatherless door.

But the framer of Life who
sees all hidden places
with his grace-studded knife
adds to what he replaces.

So that what should be lost
and deformed at its birth,
at irreplaceable cost, gains
unimaginable worth.

The rhythm of life and
the need to appease
brought the man to his wife
and his wife to her knees.

And the second wound lay
like a mask on the heart;
hoping love, should it stay,
would provide a fresh start.

And through Grace, undeserving
blooms a sapling of trust
grafted tight for preserving
as they learn to adjust.

But the cry of the loon was
not heard by another
and the heat of the moon
pushed aside every other.

And the second wound cut
far more deeper it reads
and the blood fills the ruts
as the little bird bleeds.

"Strike the king from his throne",
cry the peasants in chorus.
"Repossess all he owns,
burn the sacred thesaurus

for surely his tongue
has devised his own gallows
and each bow he has strung
doth profane what he hallows."

Let the heralds announce
and all dutifully hear,
fain mispronounce what
is painfully clear,

that the love of the maker
to restore what is broken
will in every lawbreaker
invest the sweet token

of a third wound to kill with
the power of healing;
all things empty to fill,
all things standing to kneeling.

A strong hand will extend
with a firm, loving glance
and all pretense will end
each new step of the dance.

APPENDIX

1. The Great Keeper 5.5.2016
I took a walk while visiting my sister in southern Oregon. I came upon a unique tree which looked to be dead on one side and living on the other.

2. To Build a Wall 6.6.2017
I owe inspiration for this poem to Donald Trump and the fear based instruction I received from my religious clan.

3. My Mother's Wood 2.17.2017
I was raised with an over estimated value of what others might think of us, as a family. Very early, I sensed that my feelings should be no determiner as to how I acted. There existed for me two very clear realities; one inside of me and one for others around me.

4. The Front Door 3.23.2017
Closed doors have always represented to me the greatest sense of horror and mistrust.

5. Crossroads 4.20.2017
Although products of their generation, my mother and father were desperately different from each other.

6. The Planter 6.22.2016
I inherited my emotional backpack from my parents who, in turn, inherited theirs.

7. Two Lighthouses 5.5.2017
I grew up watching two girls, my sisters, process the pain of missing their father. I also have three daughters.

8. The Night Watches 10.31.2016
My grandfather, mother and father were preachers.

9. Blind Eyes Still Cry 6.2.2017
Mark 10:46

10. The Knowing and Believing 5.2.2017
Road trips and travel were always apart of my life. I know my parents
had many occasions to travel long distances.

11. The Locksmith 7.6.2016
There have been very unique individuals in my life that have opened my
eyes
to the pain and not just the addiction.

12. Drawbridge 6.3.2016
King Arthur was always a favorite of mine. The castle and drawbridge
are strong images capturing my imagination.

13. Who Can Say? 2.16.2017
Without a healthy doubting mechanism I find the acquisition of truth
shallow.

14. Fool of the Moon 8.7.2016
In the dark, with the witness of the moon, my heart has fainted from its
stronger objectives.

15. Mountain Laurel 5.20.2017
As much as I have planned for my life and pursued my dreams, it has
been the little surprises and heartaches and small turns in my story
that have provided the clearer direction.

16. Three Leaves 11.13.2016
The miracle of chaos provides the backdrop for the sweeping arms of
love to embrace every thought and occasion.

17. The Threefold Healing 3.5.2017
Each deep and true hurt comes in threes.